Tony
PUPI
& MOVING TOYS

A fUN BOOK

Kaye & Ward · Kingswood

HAT MAN. Cut a squeezy bottle to the size shown in the diagram. Measure 50 mm from the ridge of the bottle and cut a slot up to this mark wide enough for a strip of card to go through.

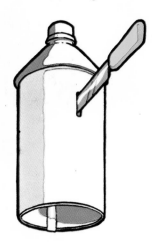

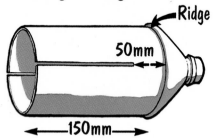

Ridge

50mm

150mm

Cut a slot in the same way on the opposite side of the bottle.
Leave 25 mm of the slots open for arms. Stick adhesive over rest of slot.

25mm

Glue paper round bottle and colour with felt tip pens.
Poke arm slot through.

Cut a strip of card 200 mm long and just wide enough to go through the neck of the bottle.

200mm

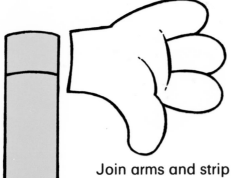

Trace, cut out and colour the arms and hands. Make a hole in the end of each arm and in one end of strip.

Join arms and strip with a paperclip and check arms move freely.

You can make a hat from the top of a spray can. Draw round the top on a piece of card.

Cut out the circle. Save the circle you have cut. Cut a larger circle around the hole to make a hat brim.

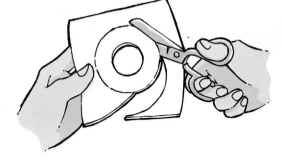

Push the top through the hole in the hat brim. Paint the hat.

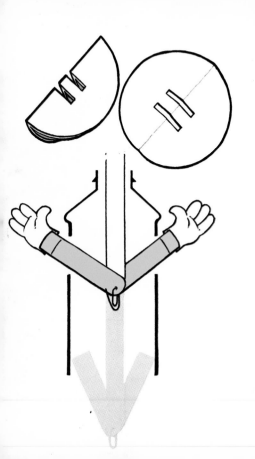

Fold in half the small circle
cut from the hat brim and
cut two slots as shown.
Slide strip through the
neck of the bottle and
the arms through the
slots.
Stick the hands to the arms.
Slot the long strip through one of
the cuts in the small circle.

Push the strip down until the arms are right up. Slide the circle about 20 mm up the strip. Fold the strip and tuck it into the other slot as shown. Push the circle up inside the hat.

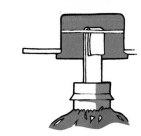

Now when you lift the hat the arms will move.

PUPPET. Trace all the
pieces of puppet onto a card.

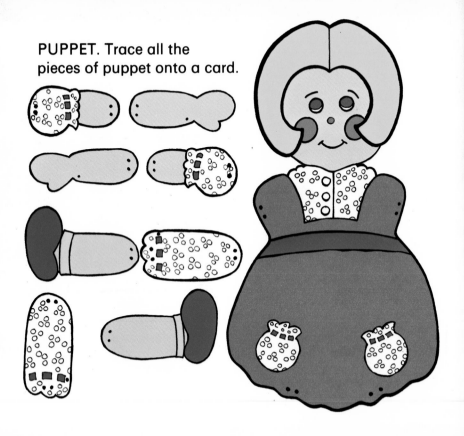

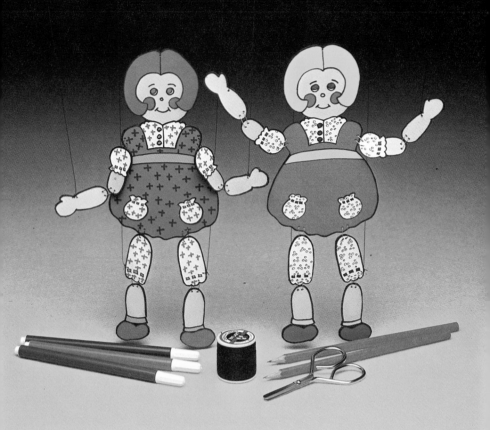

Colour and cut out all the pieces.

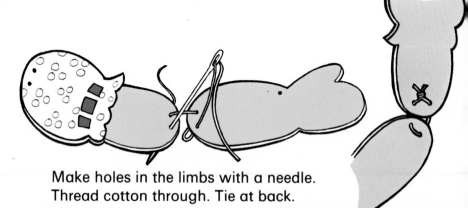

Make holes in the limbs with a needle.
Thread cotton through. Tie at back.

Tie one end of a
piece of cotton to
the holes just
behind the thumb.

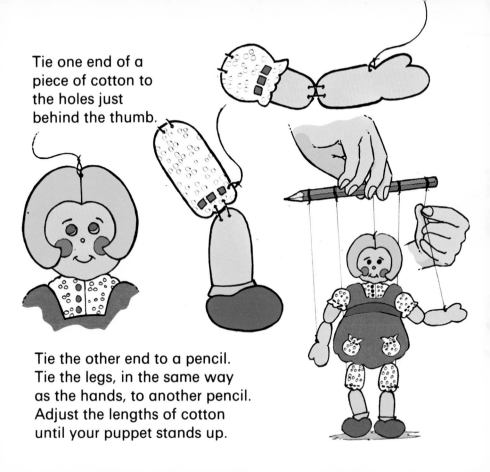

Tie the other end to a pencil.
Tie the legs, in the same way
as the hands, to another pencil.
Adjust the lengths of cotton
until your puppet stands up.

MOON ROVER
To make a moon rover you will need:
coloured paper, a glue stick, 4 cotton reels,
2 pencils, elastic bands, 1 ping-pong ball.

Cut a squeezy
bottle to the length
shown in the
diagram. Find the
seam of the bottle.
Cut a strip of card
18 mm wide and
150 mm long. Mark
a line 25 mm from
each end of the
strip of card.

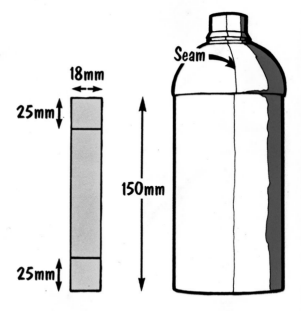

Line up the edge of the card
with the seam of the bottle.
Make a mark on the bottle
at the end of both lines on
the card. Move the card to
the seam at the other side
and repeat. This gives you
equal spacings for the axles.

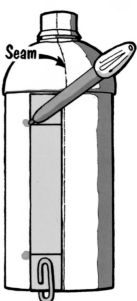

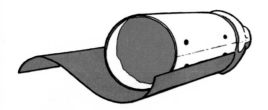

Make holes large enough for
a pencil to go through, with
a nail or a knitting needle.
Stick coloured paper round the bottle with
a glue stick. When the glue is dry make the
axle holes and trim at the cut end of the bottle.

Trace and colour the details. Cut them out and stick them to the body with a glue stick.

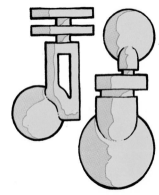

Stick strips of coloured paper to the curved top of the bottle for windows.

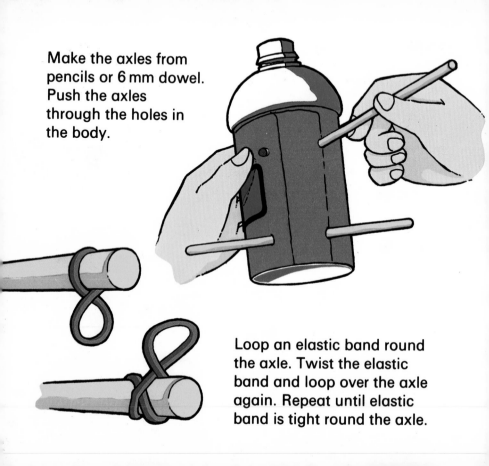

Make the axles from pencils or 6 mm dowel. Push the axles through the holes in the body.

Loop an elastic band round the axle. Twist the elastic band and loop over the axle again. Repeat until elastic band is tight round the axle.

Push the elastic band down the axle – this will stop the wheel rubbing the body. To make a wheel, clean a cotton reel and stick black paper to it as shown.

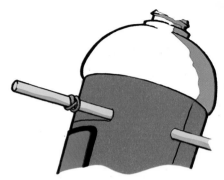

Slide the wheel onto the axle. Wind another elastic band round the axle to stop the wheel falling off. Make the other 3 wheels in the same way.

Make a hole in a ping-pong ball with a large
nail or the point of the scissors. Knot an
elastic band round a used matchstick as shown.

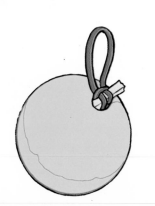 

Break the match-
stick in half. Push
it into the ping-
pong ball leaving
elastic hanging out.
Join on more
elastic bands as
shown.

To hold the ping-pong ball in place make two
cuts 5 mm long at the back of the model and
hook an elastic band through them. Push the
joined elastic bands through the neck of the
bottle. Pull back elastic band and fire.

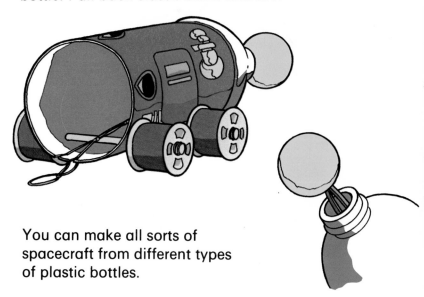

You can make all sorts of
spacecraft from different types
of plastic bottles.

SNEAKY SNAKE. Make tracings of snake and frog. Carefully mark positions of all the holes. Transfer the tracings to card. Colour and cut out.

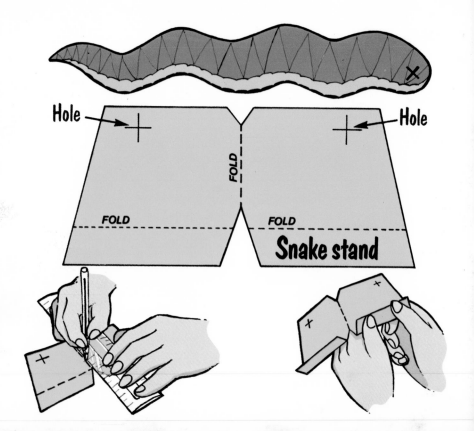

Hole

Hole

FOLD

FOLD

FOLD

Snake stand

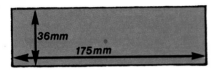

Trace the stands onto card and cut out. Score along dotted lines and make folds. Make holes with a nail where crosses are marked.

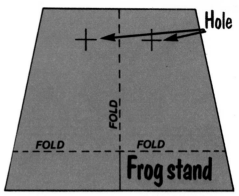

Cut a strip of card to the dimensions shown.
Stick the stands onto the card as above.

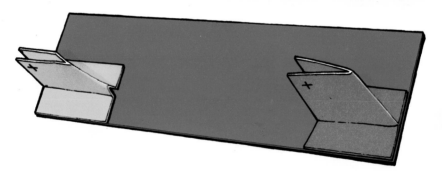

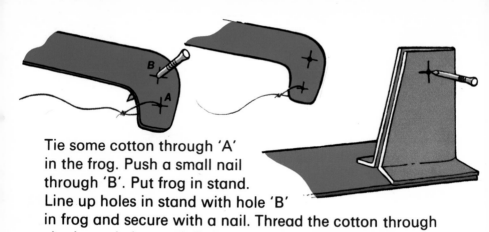

Tie some cotton through 'A'
in the frog. Push a small nail
through 'B'. Put frog in stand.
Line up holes in stand with hole 'B'
in frog and secure with a nail. Thread the cotton through
slot in snake's stand. Pull and check that frog jumps.

Thread cotton from the frog through 'C' in the snake and tie once.

Pivot the snake with a small nail through hole 'D' as you did for the frog. Adjust length of cotton so that the frog jumps just before the snake can reach it.

Remove the snake from the stand and knot the cotton. Tie the snake's tail through hole 'E' with cotton.

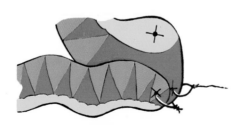

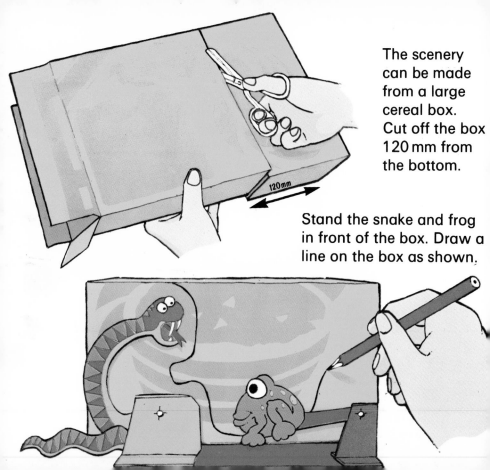

The scenery can be made from a large cereal box. Cut off the box 120 mm from the bottom.

120 mm

Stand the snake and frog in front of the box. Draw a line on the box as shown.

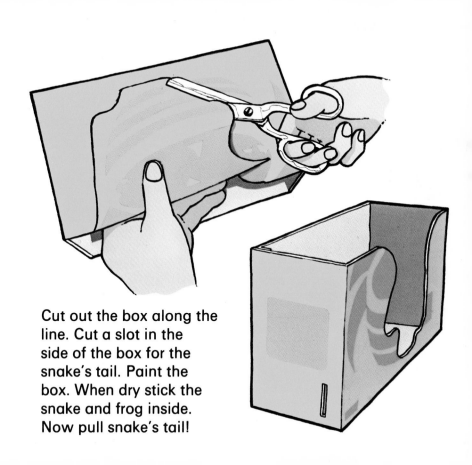

Cut out the box along the line. Cut a slot in the side of the box for the snake's tail. Paint the box. When dry stick the snake and frog inside. Now pull snake's tail!

Designed by Charles Mills
Produced by Stuart Fiddes and Carnan House

First published by

Kaye & Ward Ltd
The Windmill Press
Kingswood
Tadworth, Surrey

ISBN 0 7182 2951 7

Printed in Great Britain by Springbourne Press Ltd